KIDS ARE PEOPLE TOO

Mrs. Latischa Wells
and
Mr. Marlon Wells

Acknowledgment

Writing this book, "Kids Are People Too," has been a profound journey that aimed to shed light on the challenges faced by children in today's dynamic and demanding world. It is with immense gratitude and appreciation that we extend our acknowledgments to those who have contributed to the creation of this resource.

First and foremost, we would like to express our sincere thanks to the parents and families who generously shared their experiences, insights, and coping mechanisms. Your openness and willingness to discuss the often-overlooked topic of children's mental health has been instrumental in shaping this book.

We want to extend our appreciation to the professionals and experts in the fields of psychology, education, and child development, whose research and knowledge has provided a solid foundation for the information presented in this book. Your dedication to understanding and addressing the complexities of children's mental health is commendable.

A special thanks to the children who bravely shared their stories, reminding us that every child is unique and deserving of understanding, support, and care. Your resilience and courage serve as an inspiration to us all.

We are grateful to the readers who will embark on this journey with "Kids Are People Too." Your commitment to learning and understanding the challenges faced by children is crucial in creating a supportive and compassionate environment for the younger generation.

Finally, we want to express our gratitude to the entire team involved in the production of this book, from editors to designers, whose expertise has transformed the vision into a tangible resource.

In the spirit of collaboration and shared responsibility, let us continue to work together to prioritize the well-being of our children. "Kids Are People Too" is not just a book; it's a call to action, an invitation to dialogue, and a reminder that every child deserves a nurturing and supportive environment.

Thank you for joining this important conversation.

Table of Contents

Dedication

To our children, thank you for being patient with us. We love you all. To our Grandchildren, you guys inspire us, to be great. May you find the courage, joy, and love contained within these pages. We will advocate for you forever. We love you all.

To every child who faces the challenges of growing up in a world that can be both demanding and dynamic, this book is dedicated to you. Your strength, resilience, and unique spirit inspire us to create a world where your mental health is a top priority.

To the parents and families navigating the complexities of raising children, especially those dealing with mental health issues, this dedication extends to you. Your unwavering love, understanding, and commitment are the cornerstones of support that children need as they navigate the intricacies of life. To the professionals and experts dedicating their lives to understanding and addressing the diverse mental health needs of children, this dedication is for you. Your expertise and dedication contribute immeasurably to the well-being of the younger generation.

To the readers who embark on the journey of "Kids Are People Too," may this book serve as a guide, a source of insight, and a catalyst for positive change in the way we perceive and support the mental health of our children.

This dedication is a heartfelt acknowledgment of the collective effort required to create a world where every child is seen, heard, and provided with the tools to flourish. Together, let us continue the important work of nurturing the well-being of our children.

Finally, to us. We are both grateful and blessed to have each other, and to grow without question.

Peace, Love, and happiness to all.

Introduction

Parenting is a challenging task for many parents around the world. What matters in the end is ensuring that your child feels supported at every stage of life and development, especially in today's harsh and challenging world.

Approximately 15% of young people aged 10-19 experience some form of mental health illness. Growing educational stress, peer pressure, and domestic violence are commonly recognized as factors provoking mental health crises among children.

There are over 200 classified forms of mental health issues that can arise in children, and often, they go unnoticed until they reach a severity that provokes extreme actions, such as violence.

Parents should never shy away from seeking professional intervention to address their child's mental health issues. However, parents can also employ certain home-based coping mechanisms to help alleviate the mental pressure faced by children.

Negative behavior from a child does not always indicate behavioral problems. More often, the child may be dealing with mental health issues or learning disabilities. Mental health issues are frequently kept a secret within the household. However, discussing them is crucial, as it is the only way to help and protect our children, ensuring they receive proper care. Discussing the situation with physicians, doctors, and other professionals is essential.

Some parents feel embarrassed or ashamed of what people might say or think. However, protecting our children and ensuring they receive proper care is key to meeting a child's needs. Recognizing red flags, such as changes in behavior, isolation, and bedwetting, indicates that something is wrong. Reaching out for help and employing the coping skills mentioned above is just the beginning of accepting your child as they are.

As parents, we must educate ourselves on mental health within children. Providing proper awareness to our children will help them feel better about their conditions and understand the importance of speaking up when things are not all right. Read further to gain insight and advice on what can be done to properly support children impacted by mental health issues.

Deep Breathing Exercises

Deep breathing is one of the best ways to cope with mental health related issues faced among children. It instantly sends signals to our brain to calm down and relax, neutralizing all the negative energy and mental pressure that might have built up. Deep breathing exercises can be practiced anytime and anywhere, making it practical for parents to practice them with a child.

Experiencing mental health-related issues is not a taboo. It's like any other disease or illness one might face. In the millennial era, a rise in the cases of overall mental health issues has been noticed due to several factors. Toxicity, hate, and violence in our surroundings are on the rise, particularly in school  settings. In today's world, children face challenges due to its dynamic and fast-paced nature, which is difficult to match and maintain.

Tension is one of the main factors contributing to the growing mental health issues among the younger generation. According to psychology, "Stress can be defined as any type of mental change that causes physical, emotional, or psychological strain."

Since all humans experience stress, its management should be exercised as the main ingredient of mental and physical well-being.

Unfortunately, stress management is not widely accepted in the young generation, especially in children. By the time kids grow up or gain awareness, their mental health has already deteriorated severely, leaving a long-term mark on their lives.

Research has proven that the human brain associates different feelings and emotions based on different breathing patterns. Thus, the human brain can be tricked to alter the emotional state, preferably from a disturbed state to a stable state. Notice that when a person is happy, respiration is regular and steady. Whereas, when a person is anxious or nervous, respiration is shallow, irregular, and inconsistent. The catch here is that whenever you feel sad or stressed, try to control your breathing, making it more stable, deep, and regular to deceive the brain into thinking that everything is alright. After a few minutes of such regular breathing, you will notice that your emotional state is improving. However, control of incoming thoughts, especially those that were creating the instability in the first place, should also be tamed so that the cycle of emotional stability doesn't deteriorate once again.

Belly Breathing:

1. Find a comfortable, flat space and lie down.

2. Place one hand on the chest and the other on the ribs.

3. Inhale through the nose, ensuring the chest remains still while the belly is forced to move outward.

4. Exhale through the mouth, forming your lips in a position as if you are trying to whistle (Pursed lips).

5. Now, repeat this technique at least 5-10 times.

Mindful Diaphragmatic Breathing:

1. Position yourself comfortably on a chair or a flat surface.

2. Close your eyes and concentrate on your breathing pattern, pace, and depth of breathing.

3. The purpose of monitoring your breathing is to ensure whether you are breathing properly or stressfully.

4. If you are not breathing deeply enough or not steadily, adjust it to make it deeper and steadier.

5. The mind will start relaxing once you inhale and exhale deeper and steadier; just be consistent.

Counted Breathing:

1. Place your tongue on the roof of your mouth, breathe through your nose, and inhale for 5 seconds.

2. When you're ready to exhale, exhale through your mouth for 8 seconds.

3. Now, repeat this breathing exercise several times to relax with each breath.

4. The 4-7-8 pattern of counted breathing is another similar technique in which you inhale for 4 seconds, hold your breath for 7 seconds, and exhale for 8 seconds.

Balloon Breathing:

Yes, you heard it right; you'll have to consider yourself a balloon being inflated in this breathing technique. This breathing mechanism is centered around imagination and visualization. Start by inhaling and exhaling slowly during this respiration.

Imagine that you're a balloon being inflated, and the balloon can be your favorite color. Once the balloon is fully inflated, release it, and now it's ascending towards the beautiful blue sky.

Monitor the balloon's ascent while inhaling and exhaling deeper and more slowly. Repeat several times to get the desired result.

You're Not Breathing Properly:

Respiration is an element that cannot be skipped, and the process of breathing in and breathing out is a constant part of our existence and survival. How ever, it can also be used to control brain activity, such as controlling high levels of anxiety. Deep breathing is one of the easiest, most convenient, and most natural ways of combating issues like stress, anxiety, high blood pressure, and pain. Thus, the emphasis will remain on breathing deeper, consistently, and steadily.

Proven Benefits of Deep Breathing:

From reducing stress and anxiety to enhancing cognitive function and promoting overall cardiac health, the practice of intentional, deep breaths offers a wealth of life changing outcomes. Here are some facts explained in detail about the proven benefits of deep breathing.

Tackling the Release of Stress Hormones:

When a human being is stressed, the brain releases stress hormones known as "cortisol." These hormones slow the breathing process, decrease blood flow, and increase the heart rate, leading to heightened anxiousness. Deep breathing, on the other hand, has the opposite effect on the body. When breathing is more frequent, stable, and regular, endorphins are released. This results in smoother blood flow, a slowed heart rate, and a positive impact on the body, countering the effects of cortisol stress hormones.

Relieving Pain:

Deep breathing initiates the release of endorphins in the body, thereby relieving pain and leaving behind a soothing effect on the mind.

Detoxifying the Body:

The body contains certain toxins that must be removed. Seventy percent of these toxins are released through breathing, and the remaining 30% are eliminated through the bladder and bowel processes. When toxins are removed, the lymphatic system is stimulated, and the brain releases chemicals that improve mental health.

Breathing Improves Immunity:

Deep and consistent breathing enriches the blood with vitamins and nutrients. The more the body oxygenates, the less prone it is to illness.

Miscellaneous Benefits:

Extra Energy*:* Deep breathing brings additional energy to the body. The more oxygen in the body, the better it functions.

Organ Functionality*:* Longer breathing improves the functionality of organs, especially the intestine, addressing digestion problems.

Posture Improvement*:* Notice the lengthening and straightening of your spine when you breathe. To breathe to the maximum limit, the lungs take up more space, and your diaphragm pulls down. This helps correct bad postures that develop due to poor sitting habits.

Working Together

Families, according to sociology, are dynamic and independent units that strive to gain stability and balance. The existence of a child facing mental health issues in this unit tilts the stability equilibrium negatively. This revelation of mental health issues in the child is often perceived as traumatizing by the family, as they fear the impending societal pressure.

Due to this, parents often delay seeking professional intervention from concerned doctors. Instead of accepting the crisis,

they try to conceal it, leading to a gradual increase in the severity of the mental health crisis in their child.

Red Flags for Parents:

Whenever a child or adolescent faces mental health issues, they may exhibit various symptoms. Parents have the responsibility to identify and address these red flags.

Mental health issues in children are often expressed through disruptive, hyperactive behaviors, and behaviors concerning violence, such as:

- Breaking anything in front of them

- Fidgeting

- Problems concentrating or sitting for too long

- Preferring isolation, sitting alone, or communicating less

- Absent-mindedness or getting lost

- Emotional breakdowns, crying, or appearing sad

- Engaging in unnatural behaviors for their age group

Each of the above actions can have long-term effects on your child, negatively impacting their ability to learn, build relationships, and communicate effectively.

Parents, in this regard, should first sideline and ignore any societal pressure and build acceptance towards their children.

How Can Parents Contribute?

Acceptance is the first step in addressing and resolving the mental health state of your child. Clear your own heart; accept that your child is undergoing mental health issues.

It's not your fault that your child is experiencing any such issue. Remove any feelings of guilt, fear, grief, and stress because it's a natural phenomenon and not due to any fault in parenting or upbringing. 

Spend maximum time with children experiencing mental health issues and learn about the crisis they are undergoing. Study and perform research to understand your child's actions. However, don't compromise on your own health and mental state in this regard; work smartly.

Consult with your physician and design coping methods for your child. Apply them and create a routine that revolves around these coping mechanisms.

Look for behavioral changes in your child, such as preferring isolation, not communicating much, showing aggression or violence, or getting lost in deep thoughts. These are common symptoms that depict mental health issues. In this regard, a journal or diary can be created to note all the progressions taking place in your child's life.

Keep communicating so that your child knows that he/she can approach you whenever going through any mental breakdown. Listen to them with love and affection. Everything they say is linked to their problem; understand and analyze it to decode things.

Create a safety bubble. Don't let anyone torture your child through negative words or criticism. Create an imaginary bubble of protection around your child, keeping them away from bullies and societal pressure; the effects of which can further traumatize the entire family as well as the mental health of the affected child. Moreover, teach and practice anti-bully Standard Operating Procedures (SOP)/drills with your children so that they know exactly how to address bullying instead of absorbing everything for months and getting mentally crushed by the statements and actions of the bully.

Monitoring and Record-Keeping

Monitoring and record-keeping are key components of a healthy mental health management plan. Record-keeping becomes crucial, when seeking professional intervention from health care professionals. Doctors can analyze and convert raw information into useful data that can aid in better treatment for the child.

A diary can be formulated and maintained by parents with the following sections:

- Improvements or deterioration in mental health
- Weekly activity report
- Activities that trigger mental health issues
- Types of unusual activities
- What triggers these activities?
- What is the child's reaction to the trigger?
- How often does this happen?
- What makes your child happy?
- Useful coping mechanisms
- Parental opinion - Include your opinion as a parent regarding the observed behaviors and triggers.

Keeping a detailed record in these categories will provide valuable insights for, both, parents and healthcare professionals, contributing to a more effective management and understanding of the child's mental health.

Parent's Own Mental Health

When taking care of a child with mental health issues, parents tend to compromise and sacrifice all they have for the well-being of the child. This includes sacrificing their own sleep, mental peace, commitment to the workplace, and caring for their child at home.

Additionally, they may face financial constraints due to expensive professional treatments, societal pressure, and stereotyping.

Parents dealing with such a hectic routine for extended periods often find it challenging to sustain and may experience physical and mental health issues themselves. Therefore, the following ideas are dedicated to such heroic parents:

Leisure Time: Spend time with your partner doing things you both love and, if feasible, involve your child in enjoyable activities.

Devise a Shift-Based Routine: Plan a routine that allows both parents to avoid committing and exhausting energy and time simultaneously.

Hire Professional Support: Consider hiring professional support on weekends to allow parents to enjoy going out and having time for themselves.

Remove Regret and Guilt: Eliminate any feelings of regret and guilt from your mind; embrace and support your child.

Practice Yoga and Meditation: Try yoga and meditation to relax your mind and alleviate stress.

Avoid Quarrels and Fights: Given that parents are already stressed, avoid quarrels and fights, as they can cause disconnection and negatively impact the mental health of the child.

Taking care of your own mental health is crucial for effectively supporting your child. Implementing these ideas can contribute to a healthier and more balanced life for both parents and children.

Coping Mechanism

The mental health of your child includes emotional, psychological, and social well-being. These aspects, if unstable, can affect everyday life; the way the child thinks, body language, and even academic performance. Parents are advised to guide their children through various proven and tested coping mechanisms that help regulate the build-up of negative pressure in their minds.

Mental Health Issues on the Rise Among Children:

Ever wondered why children of the current generation are more stressed, anxious, and depressed than their predecessors? In examining the concerning rise of mental health issues among children, it becomes imperative to delve into various factors that contribute to their heightened stress, anxiety, and depression levels. Such factors are explained below.

Child Development Pace:

Child development has accelerated in recent times. Kindergarten children a few decades ago were only expected to engage in activities such as painting and playing with blocks. However, the current generation is expected to handle complex classwork as well as homework, often totaling about 30 minutes. This doesn't necessarily mean that subsequent classes face three times the workload than their predecessors. To offset this increased workload, educational institutions used to plan field trips and other entertainment activities. However, these entertainment activities are also on the decline due to an educational-centric environment and competition among institutions to showcase academic results.

Grade-Oriented Educational System:

The contemporary educational system is primarily concerned with students' test results, regardless of whether they have learned anything or how academic pressure adversely affects their lives. Many current students study in class, hire private tutors, and sacrifice sleep to achieve good grades and avoid societal and peer pressure associated with poor grades.

Landing in the Wrong Profession:

The power of society cannot be underestimated. Society now influences the future and profession of students entering professional life. In certain parts of the world, there's a taboo against opting for any profession other than Engineering or Medicine (specifically in South Asia), even if the child wants to pursue singing or acting. This societal pressure forces them into an unfavorable profession, impacting their entire life and relegating their true talents or skills to mere side hobbies.

Children's Exposure to Adult Life:

Thanks to media saturation and social media, children now have access to the adult world, affecting their developmental cycle significantly. This exposure often goes unnoticed by parents, allowing children to access explicit content that is sexual, violent and disturbing in nature.

Materials that can impact their mental state. Moreover, a wave of glamour, materialism, and luxury dominates the minds of the younger generation. Children develop an inferiority complex at a very young age, comparing themselves to influencers' artificial glamour and resources. This creates feelings of remorse as they question why they can't acquire and enjoy such luxury. In other words, young people want to skip the struggle and reach the apex immediately. When they face the realities of life and don't achieve the luxury they see online, they become depressed, and their mental state is affected.

Crisis Within the Family:

Issues within the family, such as divorce, parental deployment, or death, play a significant role in altering the mental health of children. The divorce rate in the contemporary world has seen a rise, with 1.5 million children living with divorced parents each year. Moreover, parents dislocated from their children due to deployment or work commitments pose a serious threat to the children.

Parents are the primary source of learning and love for children. When this bond breaks due to distance, children feel they are on their own, facing the rigors of the world solo. They have no one to share their feelings with, as sharing sorrows with peers or family could lead to gossip, mockery, or even bullying.

Coping Mechanisms to Improve Mental Health

Coping mechanisms play a critical role in enhancing mental health and well-being by providing effective and constructive strategies to handle life's challenges. These coping mechanisms can be used to improve mental health.

Productive Activities:

Engage in productive activities such as arts and crafts, board games, reading comic books, and any activity involving nature. These activities can be helpful for children experiencing mental health issues.

Stay Connected:

Communication is key with your child. Avoid leaving them isolated for too long. Share empathy and emotional support consistently.

Deep Breathing:

Focus on and monitor your breathing. This can instantly decrease internal pressure as the brain receives a signal to calm down and relax, generating positive feelings.

Diet and Sleep:

Maintain a healthy diet and prioritize sufficient sleep. Dehydration or hunger can lead to crankiness and irritation, impacting mental well-being.

Avoid Too Much Secrecy:

Limit secrecy, especially with individuals concerned or linked to your child, such as teachers or peers. Informed individuals can act accordingly to assist the affected child, particularly in educational institutions.

Guided Imagery:

Take mental vacations through guided imagery. Imagine yourself in a desired place, filling it with details like the sound of waves, chirping seagulls, and the scent of the ocean. This imaginative escape can release endorphins, easing stress and frustration.

Meditation:

Meditation is a proven coping mechanism for mental health issues. Choose a meditation type that suits your personality and preferences.

Progressive Muscle Relaxation:

Focus on gradually tightening and releasing each muscle in your body. Starting from the top and moving downward, this practice helps identify and release tension over time.

Walks:

Take walks in soothing spots like well-vegetated parks or peaceful roads. Play your favorite songs, maintain a slow pace, and enjoy the scenery. Change of environment can bring peace to your child's soul.

Tight Hugs:

Physical touch, especially a tight hug from a loved one, can do wonders for mental health. Hugging releases oxytocin, associated with higher levels of happiness and stress reduction.

Aromatherapy:

Enhance psychological well-being through aromatherapy, using aromatic materials as an alternative to medicines. Certain scents can alter brain activity and neutralize stress hormones. Parents can place scented candles or aromatics in their child's room for a soothing effect.

Stress Relief Supplements:

Consider supplements for potential vitamin and nutrition deficits. Examples include Melatonin (regulates sleep), Ashwagandha (builds mental and physical resilience), L-theanine (reduces stress and promotes relaxation), and B-vitamins (lowers homocysteine levels, reduces stress, and improves mood).

Tools to Be Successful

The contemporary parenting world has become more manageable with technological advancements and assistance. Parents no longer need to worry if traditional coping mechanisms are proving ineffective. The following are proven tools.

Apps for Mental Health:

Apps, both paid and free, now aid parents in identifying the type of mental health issues their children might be facing. After identification, these apps provide awareness to parents and suggest exercises and activities for their children to cope with mental health issues. Additionally, these apps analyze audio, text, and video during planned conversations to provide precise insights into the child's mental state. Headspace, Calm, and Smiling Mind are a few examples of mental health apps.

Fidget Toys:

Fidget toys, such as spinners and stress balls, are now available to target young audiences dealing with mental health-related problems.

AI Platforms:

AI platforms like Woebot, Wysa, and Replika are available to assess mental health disorders with confidence and accuracy. Moreover, these platforms offer VR therapy for trauma and anxiety.

Herbal Products:

Herbal products, in the form of teas and edibles, are available to decrease stress and anxiety, relax the mind, and provide temporary soothing effects. Chamomile Tea, Peppermint Tea, and Kava Supplements are some commonly available Herbal products.

Role of Technology in Improving Mental Health Issues

Technology, when fully integrated with the medical field, has the potential to transform the paradigm, making treatment more accessible and effective. However, parents should remember that technology cannot replace the professional intervention their child needs; rather, it should be used in conjunction with doctor visits. The following are proven benefits of effective technology implementation within the medical field.

Easy Access:

Families in remote areas with a lack of infrastructure can access low-priced mental health services through smartphones at home. Teletherapy, involving counseling and doctor treatment via video calls, eliminates the need for underprivileged patients to travel long distances; further allowing them to receive treatment at home, canceling out transportation issues, mobility issues, and societal pressure.

24/7 Availability:

Patients using mental health apps can obtain unlimited treatments at their leisure, making the process more flexible. They can open the app at home, use tools to track and manage their symptoms and access free treatment whenever needed.

Personalization/Customization:

Technology is more efficient and quicker than physical professional help. With a few entered symptoms, the app or online services database can identify the issue and derive personalized coping mechanisms without the need for prolonged patient examinations.

No Stigma Attached:

Technology can help remove the stigma associated with mental health issues by providing privacy. Internet spaces have dedicated forums and groups where patients share their experiences, coping mechanisms, and issues, helping parents navigate their child's mental health without going public and facing societal and family pressure.

Tools for Mental Health Treatment

In history and current research, these are the most effective tools for mental health treatment. Understanding and embracing these tools can make a significant difference, creating a more compassionate and holistic approach to mental health care.

Teletherapy:

Teletherapy is a videoconference-based platform that connects patients and doctors remotely from any part of the world, requiring only basic internet availability.

For example, suppose you reside in a city in California and want treatment from a doctor in Europe. In that case, you can easily book an appointment and receive treatment without traveling, saving precious resources for other needs.

Virtual Reality (VR):

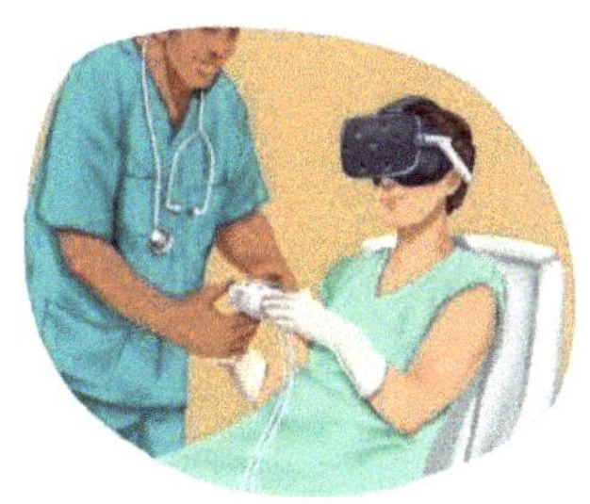

VR is a significant leap into the future, allowing patients to enter an immersive and simulated environment where doctors can assess mental health issues more effectively.

For instance, patients experiencing PTSD, such as a military veteran traumatized by past events, can be placed in a military environment to trigger trauma. This enables the doctor to identify the specific moments that trigger the issue in the service-member.

Artificial Intelligence (AI):

Artificial Intelligence in the medical domain helps patients recognize their exact mental health issues by providing a few hints. The AI platform analyzes these hints or symptoms using its vast database of information. Once the information matches pre-existing data, the AI informs you about the exact mental health condition and simultaneously devises a proven coping mechanism. Within minutes, you gain clarity about your condition and its treatments.

Kids Are People Too

This sentence emphasizes the challenging lives of children in the contemporary world. We live in a dynamic environment surrounded by technology, which has significantly altered the role of children, thereby increasing expectations and responsibilities manifold. Children find themselves in a fast-paced, competitive environment where only those focused on academics and careers thrive.

Kids Stress Management Guide:

Stress management skills for children require a complete revamp and update. Why force them to utilize outdated methods of treatment when their stress and mental health issues have evolved over time?

The Power of Penning Down Emotions: Journaling is an underrated tool for releasing emotional tension. It allows children to write down their thoughts, emotions, and experiences, providing parents insight into their stressors and triggers. This journal or diary writing is a safe and private way to encourage children to express their feelings freely. It also helps improve writing skills, rational thinking, and comprehension. Parents can encourage children

to write about positive events throughout the day to remove negativity and sorrow, and a separate Worry Journal can be created for them to pen down negative experiences.

Time Management Inculcation:

Children often experience stress when they are unable to handle their workload and routine. Time management and stress management are linked, so it's important to encourage children to be proactive and eliminate procrastination habits. This increases productivity and improves output. Teach them to set  priorities and work smartly and in an organized manner.

Develop Coping Mechanisms: Children, with the help of their parents, should devise their own coping mechanisms to tackle mental health issues.

Bullying: Bullying cannot be avoided, but children should know how to defeat it rather than being mentally crushed. Develop anti-bullying coping mechanisms at home, simulate such situations, and guide them on how to react. Reporting such incidents to school administrators and guardians is crucial.  Use online anti-bullying content for additional guidance.

Pursue A Balanced Life: Advise children to take a balanced approach in life, avoiding extremes. Devise a proper schedule that caters to their educational commitments and allows time for leisure activities they enjoy.

Indulge In Something You Love: When feeling down, indulge in a hobby—any activity done with intrinsic motivation. Whether it's gardening, photography, video games, cooking, art, or singing; commit to an activity that brings joy and relaxation.

Conclusion

This e-book aims to highlight tools and resources available to parents raising children with special needs or mental health issues. It emphasizes the role of parents as the primary support system for their child. Communication is crucial, and parents should sense in advance if their children are going through tough times. Parents raising children with mental health issues should show empathy and work together to allocate time and resources, preventing exhaustion. The last piece of advice for parents is not to lose hope, as caring for such a child is a long